42 Peaks

The story of the Bob Graham Round

Hayloft

First published 1982
This edition 2005
This revised edition 2007

Hayloft Publishing Ltd, Kirkby Stephen,
Cumbria, CA17 4DJ

tel: (017683) 42300
fax. (017683) 41568
e-mail: books@hayloft.org.uk
web: www.hayloft.org.uk

ISBN 1 904524 29 X

A catalogue record for this book is available
from the British Library

Produced, printed and bound in the EU

Contents

Acknowledgements

The first edition of this booklet was written by Roger Smith in 1982, and was reprinted with minor revisions in 1992. I am indebted to Roger for scrutinizing my revision and for his helpful comments. We are both grateful to Fred Rogerson for source material, photographs, help and inspiration; the late Harry Griffin for contributing the Foreword; Brian Covell, Phil Davidson, Maurice Collett, Des Oliver, Brian Spurrett of the Cumberland and Westmorland Herald, Bill Smith; and to members of the Bob Graham 24 Hour Club.

Paddy Buckley, Easter 2005

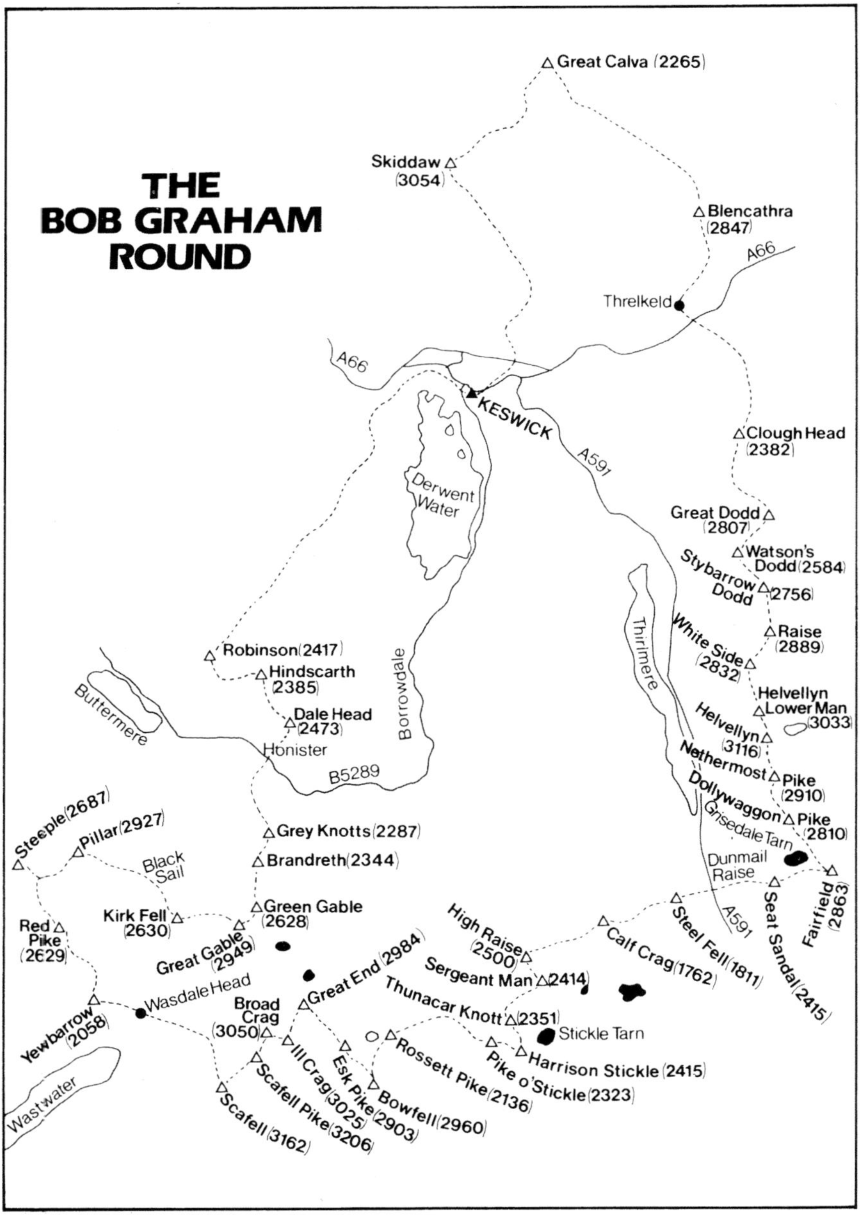

THE BOB GRAHAM ROUND
Great Calva (2265)
Skiddaw (3054)
Blencathra (2847)
A66
Threlkeld
A66
KESWICK
A591
Clough Head (2382)
Derwent Water
Great Dodd (2807)
Watson's Dodd (2584)
Stybarrow Dodd (2756)
Raise (2889)
White Side (2832)
Thirlmere
Robinson (2417)
Hindscarth (2385)
Borrowdale
Buttermere
Dale Head (2473)
Honister
Helvellyn Lower Man (3033)
Helvellyn (3116)
B5289
Nethermost Pike (2910)
Steeple (2687)
Pillar (2927)
Dollywaggon Pike (2810)
Grey Knotts (2287)
Grisedale Tarn
Black Sail
Brandreth (2344)
Dunmail Raise
Kirk Fell (2630)
Green Gable (2628)
Fairfield (2863)
Red Pike (2629)
Seat Sandal (2415)
Steel Fell (1811)
A591
High Raise (2500)
Calf Crag (1762)
Great Gable (2949)
Great End (2984)
Sergeant Man (2414)
Wasdale Head
Yewbarrow (2058)
Broad Crag (3050)
Thunacar Knott (2351)
Stickle Tarn
Wastwater
Harrison Stickle (2415)
Rossett Pike (2136)
Pike o'Stickle (2323)
Ill Crag (3025)
Esk Pike (2903)
Bowfell (2960)
Scafell Pike (3206)
Scafell (3162)

FOREWORD
by the late A. Harry Griffin

THE BOB GRAHAM ROUND of 42 Lake District fells traversed within 24 hours has been described as the most demanding test of physical and mental stamina available to British athletes or mountaineers. This souvenir booklet describes the history of this unique challenge, set up by Bob Graham's "long walk" of June 13th 1932.

My qualifications for writing this foreword are extremely tenuous. I have never been fit enough to tackle the round, but Alan and Kenneth Heaton who were the first, after 28 years, to improve on Graham's record, generously insist that it was an article of mine that inspired them to make their attempts. In the article, written when Dr Barbara Moore was getting a lot of publicity by walking from Land's End to John 0' Groats on a curious vegetarian diet, I had suggested an attempt on the long-established Bob Graham record as a far worthier challenge than the road plod, especially for mountain folk.

I knew Bob Graham, and he often expressed surprise that nobody had succeeded in improving on his round and, indeed, that only a handful of people had attempted to do so. *"Anybody should be able to do it, provided they're fit enough"* he used to say with a quiet grin. But people were just not fit enough in those days, until the Heaton brothers and Stanley Bradshaw came along. It was a great pleasure for me to drive Bob Graham, then 71 years of age, to Honister Hause on June 24th, 1960, the day on which Alan Heaton finally broke the older man's record, and to introduce him to the two brothers. When he heard the news that his record had gone at last, Bob could not have been more delighted. "About time, too" he said, for he was a modest man, not caring for the limelight.

Bob Graham, a former gardener, was running a guesthouse in Lake Road, Keswick when he did his great round at the age of 42. (He had chosen 42 fells to tally with his years.) He was a shortish, rather stocky man; hardly a natural athlete but with an excellent knowledge of the fells, a great love for the district and an enthusiasm for physical fitness. He was a teetotaller and non-smoker. He did his round, on a very warm day, in tennis shoes, shorts and a pyjama jacket. Pacers carried a pair of boots for him but he never used them. His food was bread and butter, a lightly boiled egg, plenty of fruit and sweets for energy. Years later he told me the uphill sections gave him a rest, after the jolting of the downhill runs, and recalled how pleased he felt on the last lap in the moonlight, from Newlands back to Keswick, running all the way, when he realised he was going to crack the record then held by Eustace Thomas.

The Bob Graham Round will never become a commonplace; it is far too stern a challenge for that. But over 1200 people, many of them helped and encouraged by the ever enthusiastic Fred Rogerson, have now equalled or bettered that great round of 1932 and proved their outstanding fitness and stamina. Had he been alive today Bob would have been quietly pleased, but not really surprised.

Ken Heaton, Alan Heaton, and Stanley Bradshaw with the Fell Record trophy.

The Story of the Bob Graham Round
By Paddy Buckley & Roger Smith

"This astonishing record of mountaineering skill and endurance must now rank as the world's mountain walking record".

Thus did the Cumberland Herald report a round of 42 Lakeland summits by *"the Keswick mountaineer, Mr Robert Graham"*, on June 13th-14th 1932. Graham's 1932 round marks the true beginning of our story, but it was not, of course, the beginning of record walks in the Lake District, and before starting on the story of the Bob Graham Round, it is worth taking a look back at some of the men who preceded, and undoubtedly inspired him.

Early Days

The first recorded 'round of the fells' seems to have been made by a clergyman, the Reverend J. M. Elliott of Cambridge. In 1864 or thereabouts (the date varies in different accounts) he set off from Wasdale Head and traversed Scafell, Scafell Pike, Great End, Great Gable (via Styhead), Kirk Fell, Pillar and Steeple, Red Pike and Stirrup Crag. He returned to Wasdale Head having passed over nine of Central Lakeland's highest summits in 81/2 hours.

A round more akin to the modern circuit was achieved by a Darlington man, Thomas Watson, in 1870. Accompanied by a guide from Borrowdale named Wilson, he covered 48 miles with over 10,000 feet of ascent in just under 20 hours. They started and finished in Keswick and after walking the length of Borrowdale climbed Scafell Pike (in a snow shower). Their aim was to climb the 3000-foot peaks so they cut across country to the Wythburn Valley to get down to Steel End and so on to Helvellyn. After traversing Helvellyn and the Dodds, they passed through Threlkeld, climbed Blencathra and made their way on to Skiddaw. The wind was so strong here that they had to crawl to the summit. In many ways it was an embryonic Bob Graham Round. The start and finish point was the same as today and the aim, to cover as much ground as possible within 24 hours, including principal summits, also matches modern ambitions. The '24-hour record' was becoming a recognised feat and by 1902 had been pushed up to a 70-mile, 18,000-feet round in $22^1/_2$ hours by S. B. Johnson of Carlisle. Waiting off-stage was a man who can fairly be called the first modern contender, the redoubtable Dr Wakefield of Keswick, who is regarded as the first to set out the basic rules of the challenge, when in 1904 he wrote that the aim was: -

"to ascend the greatest possible number of peaks over 2000 feet, and return to the starting point within twenty four hours."

Wakefield had developed tremendous physical fitness and stamina over many years. He used a bicycle for professional calls and swam in Derwentwater almost every day of the year. He was the first to adopt really lightweight kit on the fells, wearing a rugby shirt, shorts and gym shoes. During 1904 and 1905 he advanced the record twice. The second occasion, taking in 23 peaks, was recorded in the Sedberghian, Wakefield's old school magazine. From this account it is apparent that Wakefield would have felt quite at home on a modern BGR attempt, and it is worth quoting in detail.

Wakefield's 1905 Round

"Starting from the Market Place, Keswick, at midnight on August 14th, he proceeded along the Newlands road, paced by F. Philipson. Good progress was made; Buttermere Hause was reached at 1.18, Robinson at 1.53, Hindscarth at 2.15 and the top of Honister Pass at 2.58. Brandreth was next climbed, and by 3.58 Wakefield found himself on the top of Great Gable; this was about 15 minutes sooner than he had expected. A rest of a few minutes was taken and, on resuming, Wakefield turned his attention to Kirk Fell, paced by Mr Woodhouse. The Pillar was reached at 5.15, the Steeple at 5.32, and Red Pike ten minutes later; then the ascent of Yewbarrow was accomplished. In descending Yewbarrow he unfortunately sprained his knee. This caused him much pain and delay, with the result that he lost time steadily down to Wasdale Head. Here he stopped for 20 minutes for breakfast, and at 7 started on the stiff ascent of Scafell, whose summit he reached at 8.32; within an hour he had passed Scafell Pike and Great End. Next came Hanging Knott at 9.57 and Bowfell, reached at 10.20. From here a rapid descent was made to Stool End, via the Band, which was reached at 11, one hour earlier than expected. E.C.G. Buckley had cycled from Keswick, and after a little refreshment, Wakefield started with him for Grasmere via Red Bank (11.15). Unfortunately he parted company with Buckley over Red Bank and was obliged to go on alone; the Swan, Grasmere, was reached at 1 p.m. and a rest of five minutes was made. Next came Fairfield, the ascent of which was very trying, as there was a hot sun. The summit was reached at 2.48, and passing over Dollywaggon Pike, Wakefield arrived at Helvellyn at 4.05. A quick descent brought the walkers on to the Keswick road between Thirlspot and Fisher Place. The party then made their way to Threlkeld via St John's in the Vale. T.H. Richmond now joined Wakefield and they proceeded up Blencathra (7.25) by way of the lead mines, and the summit of Skiddaw was reached at 8.58. Halfway down Skiddaw, the pair were met by Woodhouse and Buckley, who trotted in with them to Keswick at 10.07. Wakefield finished freshly at the Skiddaw Hotel, where he stayed the night".

Eustace Thomas 1920 and 1921: new records

Apart from the section over the Langdale Pikes and High Raise, and the Dodds ridge between Helvellyn and Threlkeld, Wakefield's circuit of 23 tops was similar to the round used today, and hardly any shorter in distance. The pattern of events was similar, too; good progress early on; getting ahead of schedule; pain in the middle part causing concern and delay; the stiff ascent of Scafell; Fairfield described as 'very trying'; losing one of the support party (still a surprisingly common occurrence), and eventual triumph, with all the pacers joining the contender for the final run into Keswick. Wakefield's time of 22-07 was not eclipsed until 1920, when an attempt was made by Eustace Thomas of the Rucksack Club. Unlike Wakefield Thomas always wore nailed boots on the fells. He was a great believer in dieting, and prepared for his second attempt by training and resting in Borrowdale for seven weeks on a strict vegetarian diet. Coached by Wakefield, he covered the 23 tops of the doctor's 1905 route in 21 hours 25 minutes. The following year he returned and added the ridge running north from Helvellyn over the Dodds to Clough Head, making a round of 29 tops, which took him about 28 hours. Although this was the longest fell walk so far reported, it could not, under the Wakefield Rule, be regarded as a record. Thomas was 54 at the time.

Bob Graham's Round 1932

What kind of man was Bob Graham? He was brought up in Houghton, near Carlisle, and as a young man worked as a gardener, first in Carlisle and then in Keswick. By the time of the record attempt he was running a guesthouse in Keswick, and later took over Barrow House in Borrowdale, which is now a youth hostel. He loved nothing more than long walks on the fells, and although he also played tennis and rugby, he would not have regarded himself as an athlete in the modern sense of the word. The only training he and his friends undertook before their record round was to take regular extended fell-walks. Many of these lasted right through the night and covered considerable distances, and both Graham and his companions were obviously fit men.

Bob Graham made his first attempt on Thomas's record in 1931. Bad weather and a mistake in route finding caused the attempt to be abandoned, but this only made him the more determined to try again the following year.

There is some doubt as to Graham's age when he established his record round in June 1932. Many reports gave his age as 43, but Phil Davidson, the last survivor of Graham's quartet of pacers, stated that the 42 peaks represented one for each year of Bob's life. He also said that the extra peak added after the unsuccessful attempt of 1931 was Great Calva. This heathery hill at the 'back o' Skidda' seems much tougher than its 2265 feet whichever way you approach it, and many BGR contenders have sent a mild curse Graham's way for including it! Graham decided to go clockwise in 1932, on the advice of George Abraham the Keswick mountaineer and pioneer photographer of climbing scenes. If nothing else, this at least meant that he got Great Calva, his extra top, included early in the first section of the round, Keswick to Threlkeld.

Bob Graham, having seen to the needs of his guests, started his historic round of Lakeland summits at 1 a.m. on Sunday morning, June 13th 1932. The record attempt had been planned for the previous weekend, but had been called off because of poor weather. This time nothing was to go wrong. With Martin Rylands as pacer, the section from Keswick to Threlkeld was soon accomplished and the long ridge from Clough Head over Helvellyn to Dollywaggon Pike taken without mishap. After climbing Fairfield and Seat Sandal, Dunmail Raise was reached at 9.45 a.m. George Abraham was waiting with his camera to capture the moment on film, the photograph which forms the centrepiece of the prized Club certificate today. The next section was described in the Cumberland Herald:

"The central Lakeland mountains were climbed and crossed in the following remarkable order, and numerous new sections were added to former attempts. Mr Phil Davidson of Keswick was Graham's companion on this trying section. First of all Steel Fell was scaled, and so over Calf Crag, High Raise, Sergeant Man, Harrison Stickle, Pike O'Stickle, Rossett Pike, Hanging Knotts, Bowfell, Esk Pike, Great End to the cairn on Scafell Pike, England's highest mountain. By Mickledore and Broad Stand, Scafell was gained, and so down to Wasdale, where a 20 minutes halt was made at 5 p.m".

For the first time, this section included the Langdale Pikes and High Raise, the 2500-foot fell almost at the centre of Lakeland. Robin Deans from Aspatria took Graham over the tough Wasdale to Honister stretch, reaching the road at 9.45 p.m. They had just over three hours to climb Dale Head, Hindscarth, and Robinson, and get back to Keswick. The pacer now was Bill Hewitson, and the **Herald** records the final triumph, somewhat dryly:

"The vale of Newlands was finally gained near Mill Dam Inn at eight minutes short of midnight. The 4½ miles to Keswick were covered in good time, and at 12.39 am Mr Graham passed the Keswick Town Hall".

The stocky figure in shirt, shorts and plimsolls, jogging through the dark Keswick streets with his four trusty friends, had set a record that was to stand for 28 years. There was no great celebration; no reporters met them. They shook hands and retired to Bob's guesthouse, and at 6 a.m. he was up as usual to cook them breakfast.

Three things deserve comment. The Wakefield Rule stipulated that the peaks had to be over 2000 feet. Graham had claimed Steel Fell and Calf Crag, both well under 2000 feet, but both essential to establish the line of the Round. Secondly, some doubts were raised, certainly in private, as to whether Bob Graham had actually covered the distance and peaks as claimed. He was not that well known a fellsman, compared to Eustace Thomas and the last previous contender, Colin

Phil Davidson, Bob Graham and Martin Rylands at Dunmail Raise, June 13, 1932. (G. Abraham)

Dodgson. Had he really done it? Such doubts seem small-minded to us today, but they were genuinely felt at the time. The last oddity was not peculiar to Graham's feat but was shared with previous record attempts. The distances said to have been covered are all greatly over-estimated. The Herald report of Graham's round gave the ascent as "over 30,000 feet" and the distance as "practically 140 miles". George Abraham estimated the route as 130 miles of walking and 30,000 feet of climbing. The generally accepted figures today are 26,000 feet and 72 miles, although those contenders, who take the trouble to measure the distance accurately on a modern map, will be pleasantly surprised. Similarly, Wakefield's 1905 record was given as 90 miles and 23,500 feet of ascent. The climb is about right but the distance is again a long way out. Why was this? An error of up to 20% say, would be understandable from a newspaper reporter with little knowledge of either maps or mountains, but to be 100% out is very puzzling. Even in 1957 an otherwise excellent Herald article about long walks in the Lake District fell into the same trap, crediting Bob Graham with "well over 100 miles and something like 33,000 feet" and repeating the 90 miles error for Wakefield's round in 1905. One can only assume that the technique of measuring map distances involved string or bootlaces.

The Long Gap

Bob Graham had set a record which was to stand for 28 years. He expressed surprise in later life that his round was not repeated for such a long period; he believed that anyone fit and well prepared could do the same round. It must be remembered, however, that long fell races, the basis for fitness for many people trying the BGR today, were unknown in the 1930s, and although there were many tough walkers around, few people set out to run through the hills. F. Spencer Chapman had begun to run over the fells when he was at Sedbergh School, claiming that he could average six miles an hour.

In 1933, between his two Greenland expeditions, he made an attempt on the record, wanting to recapture it for Sedbergh. He set off from Keswick at midnight on May 17th/18th going anticlockwise, supported by pacers. He took breakfast at Wasdale Head. On Bowfell he was met by Bob Graham with hot cocoa, and on Helvellyn by Dr Wakefield with hot coffee. It was raining hard by the time he got to Great Calva, and as he was an hour down on schedule, his supporter had given up and gone home. The final climb up Skiddaw was "almost a nightmare" and he reached Keswick at 1 a.m. having taken 25 hours. In the 1950s there were several attempts, both Ted Dance and Des Oliver coming near to success but being thwarted by bad weather.

Enter The Heatons

In the latter part of the 1950s there was something of a craze for long walks. Land's End to John O'Groats (or vice versa) was a favoured route, the climax being an incredible race over this 900-mile course, north to south, sponsored by the holiday camp king, Billy Butlin. Prominent in this era was Dr Barbara Moore, an ascetic of Russian descent, who walked very long distances well into her fifties to prove that her frugal vegetarian diet worked and was indeed the optimum in calorific efficiency. Many literally followed in her footsteps, but without achieving the same notoriety.

Meanwhile, the Lakeland 24-hour record stood untouched and hardly remembered. Harry Griffin, one of the most popular writers on the Lake District and a fine mountaineer himself, wrote an article in the **Lancashire Evening Post** saying that there was nothing extraordinary in the feats of Dr Moore and her followers. Anyone could do Land's End to John O'Groats provided they were modestly fit; indeed they could get fit on the way. Now, the Lakeland 24-hour Fell Record, there was a real challenge; a time that had stood for 28 years.

The article caught the imagination of two brothers, both members of Clayton-le-Moors Harriers in Lancashire. Alan Heaton was 32 and Ken 35. Both were competent mountaineers, and both knew and loved the Lakeland fells. This was something they could have a go at. They were not alone in this thought. Maurice Collett, a 37-year-old teacher from Kendal, and Paul Stewart, a 27 year old builder from Windermere, planned an attempt on the record for May 13th 1960. It was a very gallant try; they experienced rough weather but battled on to complete the round of 42 peaks in 27 hours and 20 minutes.

Meanwhile the Heatons were planning their attempt. A back-up team of runners and supporters was organised by Gerry Charnley and a schedule of 23½ hours worked out. They decided on an anti-clockwise circuit, starting at 10 a.m. on Saturday 25th June, the nearest weekend to Midsummer Day, to give them maximum daylight. They were joined on the attempt by Stan Bradshaw, the Padiham veteran who was to achieve much fame on the fells in later years. Stan was then aged 48. The three contenders, together with Alistair Patten, who was to pace them through to Wasdale Head, left Keswick Moot Hall on a warm morning and trotted through the lanes to Newlands Hause, and on to their first fell, Robinson. Here Ken Heaton suffered an unfortunate accident. While taking a drink from a stream he took off his spectacles and another member of the group stood on them. They pressed on and reached the first road crossing, Honister Hause, at 12.12, 18 minutes ahead of schedule.

Ken decided to carry on without his glasses, but Stan Bradshaw, who had been suffering from a carbuncle on his face, was already feeling that he might not complete the round. At Honister the runners were met by Harry Griffin and Bob Graham, by now a fit-looking 71-year-old. Graham expressed the view that the hot weather was ideal (a view not shared by the others!) and wished them the best of luck. They left Honister at 12.30.

The next section is the heart of Lakeland, over Brandreth, Green Gable, Great Gable, Kirk Fell, to Pillar and then on over Red Pike and Yewbarrow to Wasdale Head, the next road crossing. Sadly, the end was near for Ken Heaton. On Brandreth he found that, without his glasses, the blinding sun was making him giddy, and he decided to abandon his attempt. Alistair Patten stayed with him as they made their way via Black Sail Pass to Mosedale and Wasdale Head. Stan Bradshaw, troubled with cramp, had dropped behind, so that Alan Heaton was left on his own. On the way down to Wasdale, Ken and Alistair met an ITV cameraman in town clothes struggling along with a heavy camera. They told him that Alan had already gone ahead, and he returned to Wasdale after filming them. Alan Heaton reached Wasdale Head at 4.15 p.m. in a bad state. He had traversed 12 of Lakeland's toughest summits at a run with no food and water on a blisteringly hot day. He sat in the shade of a car while Ken massaged his arms and shoulders with soothing cream, and the cameras recorded the scene. Alan's immediate demand had been for liquid, as he was very dehydrated, and it seemed almost impossible that he could continue. However, he was very fit and very determined, and after 45 minutes rest and plenty of fluid intake felt sufficiently recovered to go on. At 5 o'clock, 30 minutes ahead of schedule, he trotted across the fields towards Lingmell Gill for the ascent of Scafell, the longest single climb on the whole round. He was to cover the entire Wasdale to Dunmail Raise section, over 15 more summits, alone.

There was now concern over Stan Bradshaw, who had still not arrived at Wasdale. Alistair Patten and George Brass, former Three Peaks record holder, went up to Yewbarrow to meet him, and the three arrived back at 5.30. Stan had suffered further attacks of cramp, and in addition had fallen and injured his thumb on the very steep descent of Yewbarrow. As with Alan, it looked all up with him, but that was not Stan's way, and after plenty of drink and a good rest he left Wasdale at 6.25, also alone. While this drama of the fells was being played out, Gerry Charnley had managed to find an optician in Cockermouth and had got Ken Heaton's glasses repaired. They drove round to Dunmail Raise and waited anxiously for Alan. Unbeknown to them he was going well and keeping ahead of schedule. He down climbed Broad Stand on his own and crossed Stake Pass at 8.40, 80 minutes in hand. It was just starting to get dark when the anxious watchers saw Alan's white vest as he came over the top of Steel Fell and dropped rapidly down the steep grass slope to Dunmail. He reached the car at 10.53 p.m. in great shape and immediately asked for lots of hot sweet tea. His shoes, which he had worn from the start, were falling apart and had to be changed. He took the opportunity to change his socks as well and put on a tracksuit top for the night section. With Ken as pacer, Alan left Dunmail at 11.36, almost an hour ahead of schedule. He had 10 hours left to reach Keswick and claim the record.

It was a fine night and they had torches, so there seemed to be a real chance that Alan would win through. But what of Stan Bradshaw, torchless on the fells? It was an anxious two hours before he arrived at Dunmail and made the agonising decision to stop. He had covered 27 peaks, suffering repeated attacks of cramp, and come through three hours of darkness without a torch, yet was still only 1½ hours behind schedule.

All thoughts were now of Alan as the support team drove round to Threlkeld. On the tops, all was going well. The Heatons found Helvellyn well populated with people waiting for the sunrise, which greeted them on Watson Dodd. On they went over Great Dodd and Clough Head to reach Threlkeld at 4.10 a.m. Alan was still in good shape, and took only 25 minutes rest before leaving with Ken and Alistair Patten over the last three peaks. Six hours left, surely he would do it now? This last section on the anti-clockwise circuit is, however, as many BGR contenders know, a tough one. It covers 15 miles with over 6,000 feet of ascent starting with the rocky scramble up Hallsfell Ridge to gain the summit of Blencathra.

This point was reached at 5.27, a fast ascent, and the three set off on the long moorland run down to the River Caldew and the climb of Great Calva, which was reached at 6.24; leaving only Skiddaw. At that stage of the round, many people have found that a kind of autopilot takes over and energy flows into tired legs as if by magic. So reaching Skiddaw at 7.30 a.m., Alan Heaton looked down on Keswick knowing that the record was his. They came down at a fair clip, and ran into the old Market Place at 8.18 a.m. on Sunday 26th June 1960, a round of 22 hours 18 minutes. The 1932 record had been broken at last, by over an hour. It was a supreme achievement, particularly on such a hot day and with much of the toughest part of the round having been done alone. It was the end of one era and start of another. Few then could have envisaged how many would follow round the 42-peak circuit in the next 40 years.

Stan Bradshaw

A fortnight later there was another attempt. Maurice Collett and Paul Stewart, joined by Frank Caradus, were to try the round again on Saturday 9th July, and they invited Stan Bradshaw to have another crack at it with them. Although it had been only two weeks since his previous great effort, Stan agreed, and the four men set off from Keswick at exactly midnight. The weather on the first section was poor, with low cloud and rain, and on the Helvellyn ridge it was no better, but later on the day was fine. From Threlkeld to Dunmail Raise they were paced by two Kendal lads, Philip Blamire, aged 17, and Brian Berry, 16. Stewart and Caradus abandoned their attempt on Helvellyn, leaving Bradshaw and Collett to carry on. The section from Dunmail to Wasdale is possibly the most testing of the whole round, and while Stan Bradshaw kept to the schedule, Maurice Collett, delayed by problems climbing Broad Stand, found himself falling behind and retired at Wasdale Head. Stan went on and at Honister he was again joined by the two Kendal boys for the final section over Dale Head, Hindscarth and Robinson. This time there was to be no disappointment, and at 11.25 p.m. Stan Bradshaw ran into Keswick Market Place to complete the round, a tremendous feat at the age of 48 and so soon after the effort of his previous attempt.

The 24 Hour Fell Record

Having repeated Bob Graham's feat, the Heatons now turned their attention to improving the record by increasing the number of summits taken within 24 hours. A route covering no less than 51 tops was worked out and the attempt planned for the midsummer weekend in 1961, June 24th/25th. This time the support team was organised by Fred Rogerson, master builder from Lindeth, near Windermere and the man who became the compiler of BGR statistics, Chairman of the 24 Hour Club, and the inspiration behind scores of attempts. To take in the extra peaks, the start was set for the Old Dungeon Ghyll Hotel in Great Langdale instead of at Keswick Moot Hall. While training for this attempt, Alan Heaton unfortunately tore a tendon, so he had to sit it out while Ken battled over the fells. Conditions were very different from the previous year. Between Keswick and Threlkeld thick mist caused problems

Eric Beard on his Three British Tops run, 1969
(Dennis Gray)

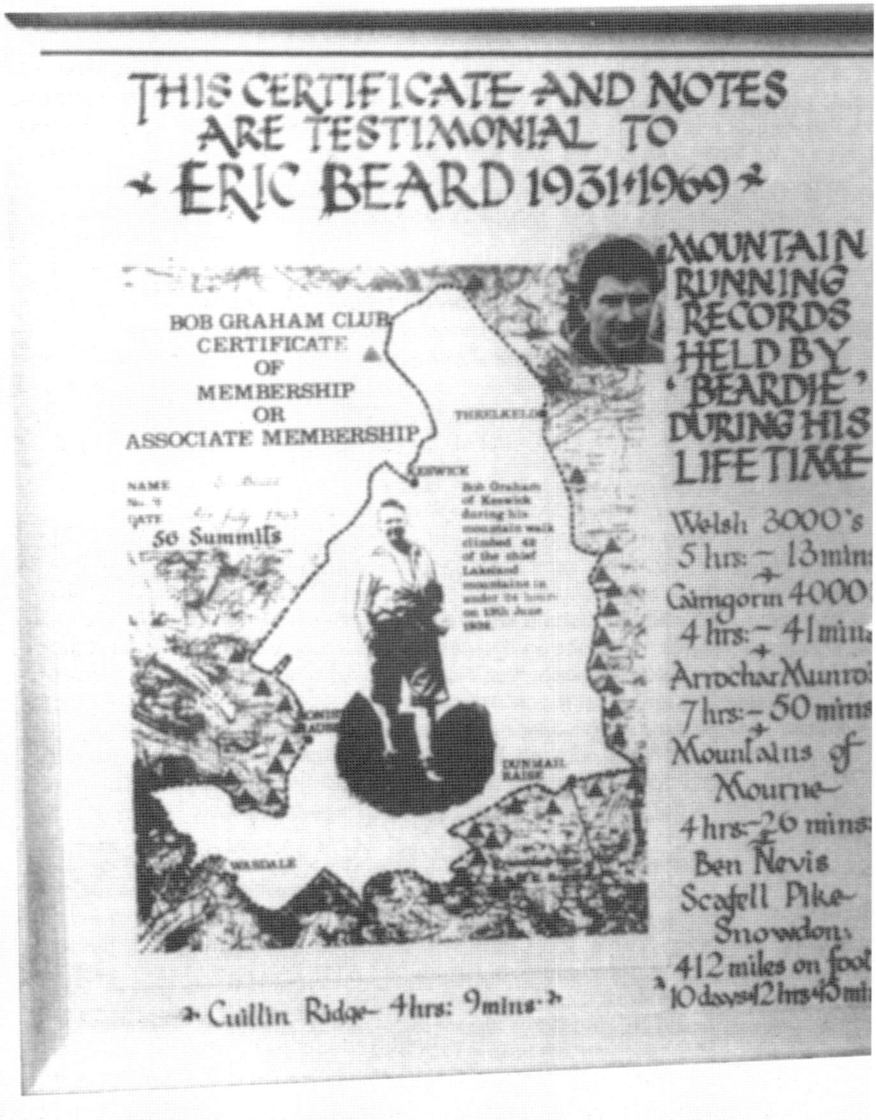

The memorial trophy to 'Beardie' showing some of his remarkable records. (F. Rogerson)

and more than once the party went astray. They had strong, cold winds during the night section on the Dodds and Helvellyn. Despite this Ken was always up with the schedule and he finished in 22 hrs 13 minutes to set a new record of 51 peaks. Ken had left out one of the original 42, Rossett Pike, and Scoat Fell was claimed as an extra, although undoubtedly it had been done by Graham, and either omitted from his tally, or put in as Steeple.

Ken had apparently put the record out of sight of any normal person. Not unnaturally, Alan Heaton thought otherwise! He was full of praise for his brother but made it clear that, provided he was fit, he was willing to have a crack at raising the record still further. And so it proved. On 4th August 1962 Alan Heaton raised the record to 54 peaks, covered in 23 hours 48 minutes. He had to contend with high winds, rain and some very slippery ground, and fell several times, once tippling head first into a bog. Despite this he was always on schedule. Alan included all 51 tops from his brother's round, plus Aikin Knott (well under 2000 feet), Scar Crag and Causey Pike. Alan had hoped to include Grasmoor and Whiteless Pike but decided at Newlands Hause to omit them in order to finish within 24 hours. This must have been a tough day, for even Alan felt the strain, as he admitted afterwards. "I wouldn't have finished if it hadn't been for the others," he said. "It was much worse than two years ago and I wouldn't like to do it again". Despite those words, he did, but not before the record had been taken from the Heatons for the first time.

Eric Beard

Next year, 1963, there was a new and rather different challenger. Eric Beard was a man who was always willing to have a go at anything. In his time he set records for most of the classic mountain rounds, including the 14 Welsh 3000s, the Cairngorm 4000s, and the complete traverse of the Cuillin Ridge in Skye. He ran from John 0' Groats to Lands End and climbed extensively in Britain and the Alps. He was a natural nomad, a wanderer to whom everyone was a friend, and he had little difficulty in getting help on this record attempt. His pacers included both Heatons, Stan Bradshaw, Des Oliver and Joss Naylor. Little wonder that he carried neither map or compass himself! Beardie, as he was always known, was 31 at the time and probably near the peak of his remarkable fitness. Although he kept his clothing as light as possible, wearing the vest and shorts of his running Club, Leeds Athletic, he chose to wear light kletterschuhe rather than running shoes.

The attempt was begun on 6th July 1963, travelling clockwise from Keswick, and Beardie got off to a cracking start, reaching Threlkeld in only 2½ hours. The next section over the Dodds, Helvellyn and Fairfield to Dunmail Raise was completed in less than four hours, including the first of the extra peaks, Great Rigg. The weather stayed fair for the rest of the round. After Aiken Knott it was clear that he would easily break the record, but instead of turning right for Scar Crags and Causey Pike, two of the tops covered by Alan Heaton, he turned left to include Sail, Crag Hill and Grisedale Pike, a much more worthy variation, before trotting back to Keswick at 5.35 on a fine afternoon with 25 minutes in hand, to complete a round of 56 summits, involving about 88 miles of travel with 34,000 feet of ascent. Sadly,

Beardie, having hitched a lift, was killed in a car crash on the M6 in November 1969.

On to 60 peaks

With the record having been taken from the Heatons and raised to 56 peaks, the natural progression was for one of them to try and get it back and to lift it to 60, a total which would have seemed quite impossible five years before. There was a two-year gap before it came about, there being three abortive record attempts in 1964, but on 24th July 1965 at 11a.m. Alan Heaton once more set off on the long trail to a new 24-hour record. Inevitably, he was accompanied by his brother Ken, and in all there were no fewer than 11 pacers. All the arrangements for roadside refreshments and clothing changes were left in the totally capable hands of Fred and Margaret Rogerson, by now almost a traditional fixture on record attempts. This time the attempt started and finished at the Old Dungeon Ghyll Hotel in Langdale, so that Alan could include Pike O'Blisco and Crinkle Crags before going on to Bowfell and the Scafell range. The weather deteriorated on Pillar and the Gables, and the party's fell craft was tested to the full before Honister Hause was reached. After covering the Newlands fells and putting in new tops on the Grasmoor section, Alan suffered hunger 'bonk' and was close to collapse coming in to Keswick. Fortunately he recovered and went on to make up time over the Dodds and Helvellyn to reach Dunmail Raise on schedule. As he had extra peaks in hand by this time, the dogleg to Fairfield and Greatrigg Man (claimed by Beardie) was omitted. From Dunmail there was only the relatively short section to High Raise and the Langdale Pikes. Alan came down from Loft Crag to the ODG to claim a new record of 60 peaks in 23 hours 34 minutes. Again he said it would be his last effort. "Seven times is enough" he said, but he wasn't finished yet.

Joss Naylor and Alan Heaton

Alan Heaton's name will always be remembered as one of the greatest fell runners of our time, and to mark his achievement, he was awarded, on January 28th 1966, the Fell Record Trophy, donated by Harry Griffin. Harry declared that the event had only one rule; - that laid down by Dr Wakefield in 1904. He added;

"There is no need for further rules, and I will always be strongly against any restrictions, regulations or special arrangements, but this does not mean that we should not quietly recognize a gallant performance when we see one. "

The trophy, in the form of a relief map of the Lakeland fells, bears the names of all record holders and after being presented to Alan was left on permanent display in the ODG in Langdale. It was later moved to the National Park Centre at Brockhole, near Windermere, where it can be seen today.

Joss Naylor

Among the pacemakers assisting Alan on the fells was a name new to 24-hour record attempts, but one with which we are to become very familiar as the story unfolds, Joss Naylor. The sheep farmer from Wasdale would not take the record himself for a good few years, but the thought of doing so may well have been sown in his mind during the Heatons' record runs. Even though Alan had lifted the 24-hour record to 60 peaks, Alan had little doubt that the total could be improved. Joss Naylor was perhaps the obvious candidate but Joss himself was not quite ready, and from 1965 to 1970 no attempts took place.

In 1970 there was an attempt, a double by Heaton and Naylor. They tried to follow Alan Heaton's 60-peak schedule and to add Fairfield and Great Rigg to make a total of 62. Why did Alan try again after his avowed intention to retire? Perhaps because he was 42, the same age as Bob Graham on the original round? Perhaps because the challenge of pacing Joss Naylor to a new joint record was irresistible? Whatever the reasons, it was a splendid thing to do, fully in the traditions of the 24-hour record, the previous holder trying to help the new man to break the record. The week before the attempt, the pair took part in the annual challenge walk round the four Lakeland 3000-foot peaks. Joss was first home, covering the 46 miles and 11,000 feet of ascent in 8½ hours, with Alan not far behind. They were ready, but the big day did not come off. Once more conditions were against them, and on this occasion the record withstood the challenge.

It had to go, however, and Joss Naylor was determined to be the next man to get his name on the permanent trophy. The attempt was set up for June 26th/27th 1971, with the start and finish at Wasdale Head, only a short way from the Naylor farm at Bowderdale. Conditions at the start were decidedly unpromising; low cloud, rain and a high wind on the tops, but after an hour's delay Joss set off up Yewbarrow, paced by Danny Hughes, and on to the Pillar and Gable fells. Honister was reached in a few minutes over three hours, a fast time and nearly half an hour up on the schedule despite the poor weather. Alan Heaton joined Joss for the traverse of the Buttermere, Grasmoor and Coledale fells and into Keswick, still half an hour up on the schedule. The next section went even better. Paced by Peter Walkington, Ted Dance and Mike Nicholson, Joss reached Threlkeld over an hour ahead of the planned time. It was as well he did, for the night section through to Dunmail Raise was again hit by bad weather. The pacers here were Ken Heaton and Alan Walker, and the three were met on Dollywaggon Pike by Stan Bradshaw and Frank Milner, bearing welcome flasks of hot sweet tea. Dunmail Raise was reached at 1.30 a.m. and after a short stop Joss carried on with Walker and Walkington to Langdale, reached at 5 a.m. The time lost during the night had partly been made up and Walker and Dance kept pace with a now tiring Joss over the last section. Alan Heaton joined them at Esk Hause and Peter Walkington took a top rope to assist with the ascent of Broad Stand on Scafell. They were back in Wasdale after 23 hours 37 minutes on the move, with 61 summits accomplished. Joss had left out one from the previous record, Lingmell, but added Base Brown and Causey Pike as extras. It was a new record and the first to congratulate Joss was, of course, Alan Heaton.

Three Rounds in 1971

The same weekend as Joss Naylor was lifting the absolute record to 61 summits, saw the first attempt for some years on the basic 42-peak circuit. The contenders were Mike Walford and Alan Evans, both from Kendal. They were not successful, but their attempt was highly significant in view of what was to happen over the next few years, and more immediately, later in 1971, when several well planned attempts to reduce the time for the basic round of 42 peaks were made. The first was on July 10th/11th. The successful pair were Don Talbot (then aged 40) and Peter Walkington (29), both experienced men who had assisted on previous record attempts. They started from Keswick together, but the younger Walkington got ahead during the latter part of the round and finished in what was then the fastest time for the 42 peaks, 20 hours 43 minutes. Don Talbot followed in a time of 22-17. Four weeks later, in early August, there was another success, a 22-44 anti-clockwise round by Michael Meath, who became, at 24, the youngest person so far to complete the round. Alan Evans started with Meath on his own second attempt, but after encountering bad weather on the Honister to Wasdale section, he retired at Dunmail Raise. Meath went on and was blessed with a fine night on Helvellyn. He traversed the final section in fine style, accompanied by Alan Heaton and Peter Bland, and finished in warm morning sunshine, to become the 8th member of one of Britain's most exclusive Clubs.

The Club is Formed

The British have a penchant for banding together, and it comes as no surprise, in retrospect, that those attempting the ultimate test of the fellsman should wish to form a Club. The initiative came from Harry Griffin and Fred Rogerson. On January 22nd 1971, at a Reunion Dinner held at the Old Dungeon Ghyll, and attended by those associated with the Fell Record attempts, the decision was made to form the Bob Graham 24 Hour Club. At its first committee meeting, on September 10th 1971, the basis for future attempts on the 24 Hour Fell Record was defined in the Club's Constitution: -

"The same summits shall be traversed on foot completely in a faster time and/or the addition of a separate summit, 2000 feet or over within 24 hours. "

Harry Griffin gave the Club due publicity in his regular column in the **Lancashire Evening Post,** and its formation can rightly be seen as the start of the modern era. In the intervening years, over 1200 men and women have qualified for membership, and many more have tried and failed. The certificate for completion of the round of 42 peaks within 24 hours is a prized possession of all those who have earned it.

The Club is 'exclusive' in the sense that you can only join it by completing the 42-peak round, or a similarly arduous Lakeland mountain expedition, within 24 hours, with your achievement verified by those who accompany you. Its greatest tradition is that of existing members assisting the contenders.

Only two more joined the Club in 1972, Ken Brooks and Jim Loxham, who got round on July 1st/2nd with just 17 minutes to spare. Tom Sykes started with them but had the misfortune to sustain a knee injury which slowed him down in the later stages. He completed the round in 24½ hours, just outside the time limit.

Joss Naylor's 63 Peaks

By then, however, the absolute record had been raised again by Joss Naylor. On a midsummer weekend of appalling weather, when any sane man might choose his own fireside rather than the open fell, Joss climbed 63 Lakeland summits in 23 hours 37 minutes, the two new summits being Lingmell and Whiteless Pike. As before, he started and finished in Wasdale. To quote the late Chris Brasher, one of eleven dedicated men who paced Joss that long day and night, "It did not seem possible that anyone could be moving on the mountains on a night like that." He joined Joss at dawn in Langdale, and prepared for the weather by putting on shorts, T-shirt, tracksuit, waterproof jacket and trousers, and a cap. "Peter Walkington, who had paced Joss from Dunmail Raise, said it wasn't enough, so I borrowed his knee length cagoule." Only a man with Joss Naylor's knowledge of the fells and instinctive route-finding could have got anywhere near the record in such conditions. It was an almost superhuman performance.

Joss Naylor and Dick Jackson

Solo and unsupported

On June 17th 1972 Stephen Poulton, a young RAF Flying Officer based in Gloucester, set off from Keswick at 1.30 a.m. on a solo attempt with no support on the fells at all, his only back-up being provided at road crossings by Shirley Hacker, who was later to become his wife. A solo attempt with companions is a daunting undertaking, and Stephen came heartbreakingly close to making it. The longer you travel on your own, the harder it gets, and on the Wasdale to Honister section the weather closed in to add to Stephen's problems. In his own words, "conditions were decidedly unpleasant for the Gables and the ridge to Honister. I was constantly calculating my chances of eventual success. They were still high provided I left Honister at 11 p.m. Ahead was perhaps the only flaw in my planning. The ridge to High Snab is slow going with nil visibility and a failing torch. I sensed my fate was sealed." And so it proved. He reached the road at Littletown with only 23 minutes of his 24 hours remaining and over four miles of tarmac to cover. There was no point in trying, so Stephen walked in, reaching Keswick Moot Hall at 2.41 a.m.

A week later, Alan Heaton made his eleventh attempt on the absolute record, starting from Wasdale on a planned 65-peak circuit. The first part of the day was very hot, but by the time night came the weather had deteriorated. His pacers made a bad navigational error on the Langdale fells and at the Old Dungeon Ghyll, with 49 summits covered in 19 hours, the attempt was abandoned. The first success of the year came at the end of July, with a triple round of the 42 by Harry Blenkinsop, Eric Roberts and Dennis Weir. Peter Walkington, already a Club member, paced the party for the full circuit, thus clocking up his second round. The following weekend four Clayton-le-Moors Harriers; Andy Churchill, John Haworth, Frank Milner and Bill Smith, made an attempt but were thwarted by extremely poor weather. Undeterred, Smith and Boyd Millen from Keswick tried again two weeks later, and this time nothing went wrong. The weather was fine and time was picked up all the way round. On Skiddaw they realised that Peter Walkington's record time for the 42 peaks was within reach. He was himself pacing them at that stage, and in the true spirit of fell records urged them on to the finish, which they reached in the new best time of 20-38, an improvement of five minutes on Peter's record.

The Bob Graham Round was taking its place as a recognised achievement for fell-runners. By 1973 there were many more regular long distance fell-races in the calendar; and more was known about training for endurance events. The 1974 season started with an attempt in early June by six Clayton-le-Moors men. Four of them retired but Roger Dewhurst and George Brass completed the round in just under 23 hours. That same weekend, Tom Sykes, accompanied by Ian Clarkson, got round on his second attempt.

Alan Heaton's last attempt

It seemed no year would be complete without an attempt on the absolute record by Alan Heaton, and on June 29th 1974, he left Lairthwaite Road End, Keswick, at 10 a.m. on his 12th try at the age of 46. His aim was to repeat Joss Naylor's 63 peak round with the addition of Fairfield and, if time allowed, Lonscale Fell, an outlier of Skiddaw. The Grasmoor and Buttermere fells were traversed in eight minutes over four hours, not bad going for a section which includes 14 summits and over 8000 feet of ascent in 22½ miles! Alan went on to Wasdale with no slackening of pace, and had still only been out for eight hours when he reached Brackenclose. The next refreshment stop was the Old Dungeon Ghyll Hotel in Langdale. By the time he got there, Alan had traversed 39 summits, travelled well over 50 miles and climbed something like 21,000 feet, in a total time of under 13 hours. By now it was dark, but Langdale to Dunmail Raise (9 more tops) still took under three hours, and the break at Dunmail was a mere six minutes. Threlkeld was reached at 6.30 on a bright Sunday morning. He had 3½ hours left to cover nearly 15 miles and top his last four summits, a mammoth task. Anxious friends and supporters waited at Lairthwaite Road, scanning the summit of Skiddaw and the ridge to Lonscale Fell as the minutes ticked away. It was not to be. As the clock on Crosthwaite Church chimed ten, Alan and his pacers came into view on Skiddaw Little Man. He had run out of time. To quote Alan "after Blencathra I just couldn't get going again." "Nobody talked of it as a failure. To cover 90 miles and 65 summits in just outside 24 hours was a superb physical achievement. This time it really was the last try. Alan's brother Ken summed up their feelings when he said "We will for a lifetime remember with pride and satisfaction each of the long days on the mountains and in the dales of Lakeland with friends and companions worthy of the occasion."

We cannot leave 1974 without mentioning two fine rounds by Peter Dawes. In June he completed the basic 42-peak round in one minute under 21 hours, the third fastest circuit to that date, and six weeks later topped that with a circuit of 52 peaks in just minutes under 24 hours. Among his supporters on both occasions was his wife Jean, of whom we shall hear much more before long.

The following year, 1975, was noteworthy in many ways. It saw the largest number of new members of the 24 Hour Club so far in a single year (14, taking the total neatly to 42); the first solo round unsupported on the fells, and a new absolute record which was to stand for 13 years. On 26th/27th July, Bill Smith of Clayton-le-Moors Harriers completed a round of 55 peaks in 23½ hours, the highest total achieved by anyone other than Alan Heaton, Eric Beard or Joss Naylor. It should be noted that, among his supporters, Peter Dawes, who a week earlier had established a record for the Pennine Way, topped 52 peaks, and Peter Walkington and Ken Brooks, 42 each!

At the end of the summer, on 20th September 1975, the second reunion of the Bob Graham 24 Hour Club was held at Damson Dene Hotel. Certificates were presented to those who had completed their rounds in 1974 and 1975 and a number of distinguished Associate Members, including Harry Griffin, Fred and Margaret Rogerson, Frank and Janet Travis, Des Oliver and Gerry Charnley, were elected with acclaim.

Stephen Poulton's second solo

Stephen Poulton, on his second solo unsupported attempt, got round with 23 minutes to spare. This time he was better prepared physically, even though most of his training, through force of circumstance, had been long road runs in flat Lincolnshire! And perhaps best of all, in Stephen's own words "I had no organisational problems with a support party, having married my previous assistant."

Joss Naylor's New Record

It had been a busy weekend for the Rogersons. Hardly had they seen Stephen Poulton arrive at Keswick Moot Hall when they were off to Lairthwaite Road to watch the start of another attempt. Just after 7 a.m. on that heatwave Sunday, Joss

Bill Smith approaching Newlands Hause on his 63 Peaks run in 1976 (Gil Horsley)

Naylor set off to try to push his own 63-peak record up to an almost unbelievable total of 72. The extra summits were to be Lonscale Fell (his first), four tops 'back of Skidda'; Little Calva, Great Scafell, Knott and Coomb Height; Fairfield, Hart Crag and Greatrigg Man, and finally Rossett Pike (missing from every previous Record since 1960). Including the last named cut out the descent to Langdale for refreshments.

Threlkeld was reached, with 9 summits already topped, in exactly three hours. One of his pacers, Eric Roberts, no mean mountain man himself, said this early in the round "he just isn't human." After a drink and a change of shoes, Joss was off for Dunmail Raise. His pacers, Alan Evans and Peter Walkington, were soon having trouble keeping up with him in the heat. Dunmail Raise (23 summits) was reached at 1.30 p.m., and a stop of just four minutes taken. Great End in the Scafell group was his 42nd summit, and he had only been out for 12 hours!
Wasdale Head was reached just after 8.30 p.m. on a very warm evening. 47 summits down, 25 to go. As he left Wasdale he was only a mile or so from his home, but the only place in his mind was Keswick. He was away up Yewbarrow in an astonishing 35 minutes (1900 feet of ascent, all at a very steep angle), and traversed the rough ground of the Pillar and Great Gable range without any slackening of pace despite the dark. At least it was a bit cooler for the body, if not for the feet! Honister came at 1 a.m., but there was no letting up. Joss still had 14 summits to top in his last six hours. He was in tremendous shape and his pacers, all very fit men, were still having trouble keeping up. The final summit, Grisedale Pike, was reached at 5.30 a.m., and from there it was all downhill, then along the road to Lairthwaite. At 6.20 he had finished. The record was shattered, with a round of 72 summits involving over 100 miles of mountain travel and 37,000 feet of ascent, a Bob Graham round and a half, all within 24 hours.

Joss Naylor's round of 72 was officially recognized at the third AGM of the Club on May 23rd 1976. But his inclusion of tops such as Little Calva and Coomb Height - both over 2000 feet but hardly outstanding summits - did not meet with universal acceptance.

During 1976 there were 13 successful attempts, bringing the total number of members of the 24 Hour Club to 55. Their average age was 34; the oldest was Eddie Hill aged 49, and the youngest Andy Lewsley aged 20. Frank Milner was sponsored for youth organisations when he did his round in May, and raised the staggering total of £100,000, which must have made his achievement feel especially sweet. The report on his attempt was written by his wife Wynne, and to read it will bring a tear to the eyes. The fastest time for the basic round had been lowered by Billy Bland to 18 hours 50 minutes. August 14th was notable for a 'triple Bland'. As well as Billy's very fast round, Anthony and David Bland also completed the circuit, in a little over 20 hours.

On July 24th/25th Bill Smith pushed his total of 55 peaks, achieved the previous year, up to 63, equalling the second highest round ever completed. He had set out basically to lift his target above 60 peaks, but secretly had prepared a schedule for no fewer than 77! However, by the middle section it was apparent that Joss Naylor's record was in no danger, and in the end Bill reached Great Crosthwaite, his start and finish point, with only five minutes in hand. It was still a very fine effort.

Just as significant, perhaps, was the year's most glorious 'failure' (really quite the wrong word). At midnight on 31st July, Jean Dawes, wife of Peter, set off from Keswick in an attempt to become the first lady member of the 24 Hour Club. She had trained carefully for the attempt, and knew the fells. She was well supported, and there seemed every chance that she would be successful. With Brian Tatham for company, Jean reached Threlkeld in a little under four hours. So far so good. For the long haul over the Dodds and Helvellyn, Jean was accompanied by Stan Bradshaw, seemingly no less fit at 64 than he had been when he completed his own round back in 1960. Dunmail Raise was reached at 8 a.m., and Stan carried on with Jean and Alan Barber to Wasdale Head. The section was completed in just over six hours, with Jean still in excellent shape. After Wasdale, she began to suffer. To quote Boyd Millen, "Off Great Gable she looked as though she had been cooling her head with flour." The time was getting tight and it was going to demand a tremendous final effort to get back to Keswick by midnight. Jean left Honister Hause at 9 p.m., very tired but determined to complete the round, even if she was outside the time. Over the last three summits she got slower and slower and coming off Robinson was literally asleep on her feet. The waiting support group saw the party's torches come slowly down, stopping several times. By the time Jean reached the road at Newlands her time had all but run out. She carried on and reached Keswick just 50 minutes after midnight. Everyone with her knew that she was capable of completing the round, and hoped she would try again.

Jean Dawes, First Lady member

An Amazing Year

Although Bob Graham always maintained that "any reasonably fit man" could complete the 42-peak round inside 24 hours, he probably never envisaged a time when women would achieve it, or young fellows of 17, for that matter. And although he had himself reached the mature age of 42 when he did his 1932 round, he might not have felt like trying again to mark his 65th birthday. Yet all these feats were achieved in a single year, 1977. There were no fewer than 33 new members taking the Club membership up to 88.

The fastest time for the 42-peak round was lowered by Mike Nicholson to 17 hours 45 minutes. Jean Dawes achieved her dream of becoming the first lady to do the Bob Graham Round; Boyd Millen achieved a double non-stop circuit; Alan Walker trotted round completely on his own, without even roadside support; and the age range of successful completions was an astonishing 48 years!

Let's get all that into some sort of order. At the end of May, Eddie Hill completed a circuit of 50 peaks to mark his 50th year, accompanied by Harry Ball. While assisting Ken Ledward to complete his round, Joss Naylor put in a bit of extra training by doing the full circuit! Alan Walker's solo round was completed on June 10th. It is quite hard enough completing the BG42 with full support on the fells and at road crossings. To do it on your own with no support is mind-boggling. Nor did Alan enjoy good weather, but that probably merely added a bit of extra challenge. The round was completed in less than 22 hours.

Jean Dawes 'First Lady' June 26 1977

Jean Dawes succeeded at her second attempt. Let us quote from her own report. "Keswick car park, 7.55 a.m. Rain. No chance to back out now, everyone's ready in their gear. Arrival of Chris Bland, 'I'll do a couple of sections with you'. 8 a.m. and it's a relief to start running. The rain gets worse on Skiddaw, then through the heather to Great Calva, a good run down to the Caldew and a long drag up Blencathra. Into the mist, Pete navigating by instinct and we hit the narrow track to the summit. We descend out of the mist and see the waiting cars at Threlkeld. I'm looking forward to that cup of tea."

All went well as far as Dunmail Raise, reached at 3.20 p.m. Chris Bland was persuaded to go all the way round, as was the 65-year-old Stan Bradshaw. Jean takes up the story again. "Weather now dry but windy. Didn't seem to take long up Steel Fell and across the Pikes. Picnic at Stakes Pass. Seems a long haul up Bowfell, getting cold, cramp in toes, take a couple of salt tablets, eat Roman Halenko's supply of butterscotch. I've been running 12 hours and I can't face the thought of another 12 hours. Broad Stand wet in places, 'slape' you might say. Rough descent of Scafell and the rest of the team catch up".

The Wasdale-Honister section is crucial to the success of all clockwise attempts, and this was no exception, as Jean inevitably began to tire. On Kirk Fell she lost her torch and took a rest on a boulder, almost falling asleep. She heard Boyd Millen say "We've lost her, where the hell is she?" and thought she had better get moving again. But all was well, and Honister was reached at 4 a.m., with ample time to cover the last three summits and get back to Keswick.

"Soup, tea and off with the Liverpool contingent, Bill and Eddie, for the last three summits. Eventually descend the rock steps off Robinson, only the road to do. Plod along the lane, not running much. Wonder where Stan is now. Final sprint up the main street of Keswick with time in hand, to lean thankfully against the Moot Hall". She had done it, with half an hour to spare. Reflecting on her round, Jean Dawes summed up the feelings of many when she said "Fred Rogerson has a lot to answer for, encouraging us in these mad but beautiful days on the fells, but when you are at the Bob Graham Club dinner you look round the room at all those runners and believe it when I say he has given us all some moments in our life which are unforgettable."

Stan Bradshaw, still plodding on after a bad spell during the night, arrived not long after Jean had finished, "coming up the street with a broad grin." He was outside the 24 hours but that was of little account to him. Five weeks later on July 31st he completed another round of the 42, this time in one minute under 24 hours, to become the oldest person thus far to complete the Bob Graham round. To do two circuits so close together at 65 years of age is an unsurpassed achievement.

Boyd Millen's double

July 31st was another notable day in the annals of Lakeland fell records. Boyd Millen, at the age of 41, completed a double Bob Graham. The first circuit was run clockwise in 21½ hours and with only an hour's break Boyd was off again on an anti-clockwise tour. This was inevitably a lot slower but he returned to Keswick in 30½ hours for the first-ever double round. The statistics are staggering, distance 144 miles; ascent, over 50,000 feet; summits climbed 84. Less than three weeks later, Boyd Millen was back on the fells again, assisting a group of three runners from Rochdale Harriers; Tony Shaw was 40 and Roman Halenko 24. They were both experienced fell runners and both felt confident that the round was within their capabilities.

Youngest Lad

The third member of the party could have been excused for having some doubts. His name was Steven Tosh and he was just 17 years old. For a year he had nourished the ambition to be the youngest person to complete the round, and now the day had arrived. It all went unbelievably well. The weather stayed fair, the party stayed together, and Steven's only moment of worry was on Great Calva when he "felt like being sick". The cure was a rest and a Mars Bar and after that there were no more problems. Steven's round was achieved in 22 hours 43 minutes and his description of his feelings at the end is well worth quoting;

"On the way down Skiddaw we looked back over the past 24 hours and agreed it had been the most enjoyable day we had ever spent. Running up Keswick main street towards the Moot Hall, seeing my Mum and Dad and all the rest who had gathered to meet us was the proudest moment of my life. It was a fantastic day, spent in the company of the finest people I know".

At the third reunion, held at Ambleside Park Hotel in November 1977, there was much to talk about. Jean Dawes received a standing ovation as well as her certificate of membership, and an engraved crystal goblet to mark her achievement. She was visibly moved. She then turned presenter and gave Stan Bradshaw a copper etching of a fell scene in recognition of 25 years of endeavour on the mountains.

As with other outstanding athletic achievements, once they have been done they are soon repeated, and in June 1978 Anne-Marie Grindley was welcomed as the

Paddy Backley paced by John North, May 1980

Roger Smith, June 1979

Sue Walsh, August 1984

Margaret and Mary, identical twins at Wasdale, July 1996

second lady member of the 24 Hour Club. Her reaction is interesting, after finishing she recommended the Round to other ladies! "All those lovely men waiting on you hand and foot, " she said. "I've never felt so cosseted in my life!" Nonetheless the physical effort is the same, and Anne-Marie's round, accomplished with her husband Will (another record, the first husband and wife team to do a round together) in just over 21 hours was a very fine achievement.

By the end of 1978 there were 110 full members of the 24 Hour Club, with ages ranging from 17 to 65, and an average age of 34. By the end of 1981, that total had all but doubled, to 212. Three more ladies had joined, Ros Coats and Wendy Dodds in 1979 and Lilian Millen, Boyd's wife, in 1980.

The Eighties

The 1980s saw a steady increase in the numbers of people taking up fell running and other endurance sports, better all-round fitness, a greater awareness of the special nature of the fell country, and not unnaturally a continued growth in the Club's membership and in the level of achievement. There is only room here to record some of the many highlights of a memorable decade.

Anniversary Celebrations

In 1982 the Club enjoyed a memorable year. In June, Club members came from all over Britain to mark the 50th anniversary of the original 1932 round. Forty of them took part in a relay around the 42 peaks. By a most happy coincidence, the relay was started by Phil Davidson, the last survivor of Bob's pacers, on his 80th birthday. Alan Heaton carried the baton out of Keswick up Skiddaw before handing it on. It passed from runner to runner all the way round until Jean Dawes, our first lady member, trotted in with it from Portinscale escorted by many of those who had carried it earlier. Fred Rogerson had worked out what he described as a "leisurely schedule" of 19 hours 30 minutes. Something must have gone wrong, for the baton arrived back at the Moot Hall a minute late! There followed a most enjoyable social at Barrow House, formerly Bob Graham's guesthouse, and the unveiling by Eva Graham of a plaque in his memory set into a cairn near Ashness Bridge.

A week later, Don Talbot marked his 50th birthday and the Jubilee with a superb round of 50 peaks in 22 hours 51 minutes. The following weekend, midsummer itself, Billy Bland crowned the celebrations in unforgettable style with a magnificent round, his second, in 13 hours 53 minutes, a time which still stands today as the fastest ever.

First overseas member

On July 2nd 1983, the Club welcomed its first overseas member, Reinhard Ackermann, a very experienced ultra-distance road runner with a great love of the mountains. It was his first visit to England, and he more or less invited himself along to join an attempt by Otto Appenzeller, John Kendall and Ken Laverick, and "with very little knowledge about what was going to happen", arrived in Keswick a month after recording his best time, 8 hours 51 minutes, for the famous 100km Biel race in his native Switzerland.

Fred Rogerson offered what Reinhard calls "some philosophical advice" and led by Tony Creswell and Ralph Stevenson off they went up Skiddaw, in mist and rain "under the wings of a support party which relieved us of all responsibility other than that over our own minds and bodies. It was difficult for me to tell where we were as we were always in rain and mist and instead of names, our leaders were calling out compass bearings; it was best not to think about the individual summits, but to follow our navigating friends and concentrate on the step ahead. This went rather well, and by Helvellyn we had gained four minutes on the schedule".

By Dunmail Reinhard was now the sole contender. "I decided to try my best, even though I had no idea of what lay ahead, and those who knew wisely did not tell me. In the Red Pike area we were met by Joss Naylor who, just through his presence, seemed to shift the whole group into a higher gear. He came with us to Steeple before dropping off into the misty depths with the quiet agility of a cougar". They reached "the beautiful VW and its teapot in Little Town" in good time and Reinhard "headed down the road to Keswick, elated and happy even though I must have shown signs of utter tiredness". At the age of 59 Reinhard became a member of the Club with a round of 22 hours 35 minutes. He was met by Tom Sykes, who had repeated Don Talbot's feat of 50 summits to celebrate his 50th birthday.

Beyond the Round

On the weekend before midsummer 1981, Leo Pollard set out on foot to link all 26 lakes, meres, and waters in the Lake District in a single expedition, said to be a distance of 105 miles with over 17,000 feet of climbing. The original run had been devised by Dave Meek. Pollard first attempted the run in August 1980, but abandoned it when he was seven hours behind schedule. This time he was successful, the first time, so far as is known, that this had been achieved. Starting at Loweswater, he finished at Overwater 35½ hours later. Leo was supported throughout but had to endure generally poor weather conditions. The 'running order' was Loweswater, Crummock Water, Ennerdale Water, Wastwater, Devoke Water, Goats Water, Low Water, Leverswater, Coniston, Esthwaite Water, Elterwater, Grasmere, Rydal Water, Windermere, Skeggles Water, Small Water, Blea Water, Haweswater, Hayeswater, Brotherswater, Ullswater, Thirlmere, Derwentwater, Bassenthwaite Lake, Overwater.

The next weekend Pete Schofield completed a similar run in 42 hours 39 mins. This set up an intriguing new challenge that was soon taken up by none other than the redoubtable Alan Heaton. On 1st August 1982, Alan followed the original route, in better conditions, with both Pollard and Schofield as pacers, in a fast time of 25 hours 17 minutes. On June 25th 1983, Joss Naylor applied himself to the Lakes Run and cut the time back to an almost incredible 17 hours 14 minutes, five minutes inside the schedule he had set himself.

People were looking beyond the basic round, itself still a great physical achievement for many people, to bigger and more demanding challenges. At the end of July 1984, Steve Parr achieved the fastest completion of a round taking in all the Lakeland summits over 2,500 feet, 61 in all, and the first in less than 48 hours. In keeping with tradition, he started and finished at the Moot Hall, Keswick, recording a time of just over 43 hours. He had a support team totalling 20 people and very mixed weather conditions. The total distance was worked out as 116 miles and the ascent as 42,550 feet.

New rounds continued at a steady rate, with 39 being successful in 1984. It was a notable year for the ladies with their number jumping from seven to 13. (Elaine Stephenson, Angela Carson, Bridget Hogge, Inken Blunk, Sue Walsh and Gill Simpson.)

The Wainwright Round

In each of the following two years, even Steve Parr's 61 summit round was to be eclipsed by what must surely be the ultimate expedition in Lakeland, setting foot on every one of the 214 summits named in the books of Alfred Wainwright. This is a noted peak-baggers target, comparable with the climbing of the 284 Munros in Scotland, but most people take years to achieve it, some indeed spreading it over half a lifetime. John Beech, a dedicated walker and international chess player, had devised "A plan to visit the 214 Wainwright tops consecutively", and had allowed himself a month to complete the task.

Chris Bland of Stonethwaite, then aged 40, was the first to take up the challenge. His idea was to do a book each day (there are seven). As a churchwarden Chris also wanted to raise money for the repair of Borrowdale church roof, and so decided to start and finish each day at a church. Chris began his mammoth task on June 27th 1981. By the end of the week he had visited 192 of the 214 tops, an incredible display of courage and stamina.

Alan Heaton was the next to tackle this huge challenge. His strategy was to revert to John Beech's original continuous route rather than the book a day solution preferred by Chris Bland. Alan set out on 29th June 1985, two days after his 57th birthday, and completed the full Wainwright Round in a total elapsed time of 9 days 16 hours 42 minutes. He spent 6 days 1½ hours actually on the fells.

It seems that whenever Alan had set a target, Joss Naylor was energised into attacking it. He had done this with the Lakes Run in 1983, and he did it again with the Wainwright Round in 1986. Joss started from the Moot Hall at 4 a.m. on Saturday 27th June. He began with the Whinlatter Fells then worked round to Skiddaw on a day of intense heat. The day ended at Dockray. The heat wave continued for four days as Joss climbed the fells of Ullswater, Helvellyn, Watendlath, Easdale, Langdale, Coniston, Eskdale, Wasdale and Loweswater. He suffered badly from the heat on this latter section. The weather then broke and he and his support team were forced to bivouac near Floutern Tarn in strong winds and rain. Conditions improved and the Ennerdale and Honister fells were duly completed. After a final stop at Newlands Hause on Friday 3rd July, the party set off for the last

15 tops around the Newlands Valley, reaching their final summit, Barrow, almost exactly a week after setting off from Keswick. The Moot Hall was reached at 5.25 a.m. on Saturday 4th July to set a time of 7 days 1 hour 25 minutes. Joss had calculated that the distance travelled was 391 miles with 121,000 feet of ascent. For this marvellous feat of endurance and navigation, Joss rightly received the Achievement of the Year Award for 1986-87.

There was another notable achievement in 1985, when 19-year-old Alison Wright joined the Club with a round in 23 hours 19 minutes, the youngest lady member. Since then Alison achieved a second round in just over 19 hours in 1990. There was much activity throughout the 1985 season, with a record 54 new members joining. As well as Alison, rounds were achieved by Vanessa Brindle and Sandra Wilkinson. But 1985 was eclipsed by 1986, with 69 new members, with just two ladies, Gillian Wilkinson and Nicola Lavery, achieving rounds towards the end of the season.

First Winter Rounds

There is normally a pause in BGR activity between September and May, allowing us all to draw breath, look back on the year's achievements, perhaps at our biennial dinner, and prepare for another year of success for some, and, inevitably, failure (though that is a very subjective term) for others. However, during the winter of 1986-87 there was a change. No fewer than four members completed midwinter rounds of the 42 peaks. This is a truly outstanding achievement when you consider that for 16 of the 24 hours you are going to be in darkness or semi-darkness, even on a good day. A mild winter meant there was little snow on the tops, but even allowing for that, to cover the distance and navigate successfully in the dark takes some doing.

The first winter round was done by John Brockbank and Selwyn Wright on 13th-14th December 1986, in a very respectable time of 23 hours 6 minutes. They were followed on 22nd-23rd December by Steve Parr, in a time of 23:26. Martin Stone dispensed with support and completed a solo winter round on 7th-8th January 1987 in 19 minutes under the 24 hours. Quite apart from the considerable physical achievement this represents, mentally it is a quite extraordinary feat. It is possible to keep going beyond the normal limits of endurance when you have good support to encourage you, but to keep yourself going, for so much of the time in the dark cold of winter, is exceptional.

In the following year, 1987, 55 new members joined the Club. Alan Barber became the fourth 50-year-old to complete a round of 50 summits, in a faster time than he had managed on his original 42-peak round! Helen Diamantides completed the first of her three rounds, in 22 hours 18 minutes, and Sarah Haines, the 20th lady, joined husband Peter as a member. The last two rounds of the year, by Andrew Addis and Paul Ramsden, took Club membership to 501. It was a good year, but perhaps without a particular spark. That was to be provided with a vengeance in 1988.

The Fell Record

The Lakeland Fell record had been the subject of much debate since Joss Naylor's epic 72 summit round in 1975. Much of the discussion centred on what constitutes a 'peak', and the Club's records reveal the arguments for and against particular criteria. Fred Rogerson had drawn up a schedule for a 75-peak round, and the first to try this challenge was Martin Hudson, who found the schedule relentlessly demanding. There were some who said it could not be done.

Mark McDermott had other ideas. He prepared a schedule for a 76-peak round, adding to Joss's list Bowscale Fell and Bannerdale Crags in the Northern Fells, plus Ladyside Pike and Whiteside. The attempt was planned in meticulous detail. Mark had an intimate knowledge, and love, of the fells, and had reccied every section by day and night. Mentally he was thoroughly prepared, and had gathered together a superb team of 25 pacers and helpers. The attempt started at 5 a.m. on 18th June 1988 from Braithwaite. In less than four hours, Threlkeld was reached with 11 summits traversed, including the two extra tops of Bowscale Fell and Bannerdale Crags. Here, in Mark's words, "the next batch of donkeys (Andrew Addis, Bob Lee and Rob Smith) were ready and laden with gallons of water and bags of food, and we set off merrily up Clough Head".

On they went over the Dodds, Helvellyn and Fairfield to Dunmail Raise, with 7 hours 20 minutes gone and 25 summits bagged. A shortish section to Langdale followed, 9 summits in exactly two hours. On Crinkle Crags Mark was asked if he was doing a Bob Graham Round. "I wish I was!" he answered. Then the big chunk of country over to Wasdale Head had to be tackled. It was done by just over 7 p.m.: 49 summits down and Mark was feeling good. He told Alison Wright "It's in the bag!" and showed "my usual combine harvester approach to food" at the brief halt. On Kirkfell they enjoyed a glorious sunset, and "feasted on Battenburg cake" on Great Gable. Honister was reached just after 11 p.m. with 61 peaks covered and six hours to go. A rapid traverse of Dale Head, Hindscarth and Robinson saw them at Newlands at half past midnight. Mark still had time to admire the beauty of the scene: "Soon we were on the ridge to Causey Pike with the moon beaming, the stars twinkling, and the lights of

Anne Stentiford, holder of the Women's 24 Hour Fell Record 1991

Keswick glowing invitingly down in the valley. The edges of the sky were still tinged red. What a night!" By the time they reached Grisedale Pike, dawn had broken and they could actually pause for photos and congratulations. Down the "painfully stony track" to Braithwaite, reached at 4.26 a.m., and a new Fell Record had been set, 76 peaks in 23 hours 26 minutes, including only 18 minutes of rest. Not surprisingly, Mark received the Achievement of the Year Award. Martin Stone's citation says that his pacers and supporters (Martin was one himself) "witnessed Mark's ruthless determination to succeed and also learned a valuable lesson, one should never underestimate a person's will to achieve nor should any record, however remarkable, be deemed unbeatable". The distance travelled was about 108 miles and the height climbed was 39,000 feet: astonishing statistics.

Billy's Wee Walk

There are always new challenges on the fells, and on 22nd-23rd July 1989 Billy Bland, holder of the record for the fastest round, but now retired from fell racing, decided to see if he could get round inside 24 hours, walking all the way. By very careful study of the map he got the mileage down to 65, and he persuaded his 17-year-old nephew Gavin to accompany him. Setting off from the Moot Hall at 7 a.m. they were at Honister by 9.30, already up on schedule. Between Kirkfell and Pillar they had to slow down as they realised they would reach Wasdale Head before their pacers. In the event they were so far ahead of schedule they sent Pete Novak to meet the new pacers, Ann and Dennis Hayes, to divert them to Esk Hause. Dunmail Raise was reached at 6.23 p.m. in good shape and there were no problems on the next section. By Threlkeld they knew they would get round easily, although Gavin was feeling pretty tired. After Blencathra, Billy "started getting fed up as I couldn't get it over as fast as I wanted". Mungrisdale Common "seemed endless" and here Billy felt the start of a blister as he was wearing road running shoes. After Skiddaw Billy went ahead, reaching the Moot Hall at 3.48 a.m. Gavin followed ten minutes later. Both of them had beaten 21 hours, an excellent time for those running the round. Billy summed up his effort.

"After running fell races for 15 years with virtually no injuries, two days after the walk I had a problem with my knee, torn ligaments, most likely caused by holding back downhill, which was the hardest part of the round. Still, this hopefully might encourage those who think they'll never be able to do a BGR to see it in a different light. Have a go!"

In 1988 the Club's membership increased by 76 from 501 to 577. In his 56th year, George Brass achieved a round of 55 summits in 16 minutes under 24 hours. Like good wine, he had obviously improved with age. In 1990 two men, Richard Lamb and Rory Longmore, each separately achieved Lakeland rounds of 61 summits.

Helen Diamantides certainly "had a go" in 1989, completing the three major rounds during the summer. She set a ladies' record for the Paddy Buckley Round in Snowdonia (61 miles, 47 summits) in June, followed that with the Charlie Ramsay Round of 23 Munros in Lochaber in July, and in August a second Bob Graham

Round in the fast time of 19 hours 11 minutes.

In 1990 there was a marked dropping-off in completions, only 40, half the total for the previous year. Three ladies, Catherine Proctor, Sue Ratcliffe and Debbie Cooper were successful, as was John Rawnsley at the age of 53. John organises the Three Peaks cyclo-cross race and claims to have done the Three Peaks circuit in Yorkshire over 120 times! In 1991 the total of new members rose a little to 52. Hilary Bloor joined her late father Jack as a member; husband and wife Neal and Jean Shotter went round together, as did Nicola Davies, and the last to complete in the year was Mark Bevan, who became Club member no 748. In July Mike Hartley set off to complete the three great British 24-hour rounds, the Ramsay, Graham and Buckley, within four days. He took the Lochaber round first, recording 21 hours 14 minutes, followed it with a BGR in just 12 minutes under 24 hours and then drove down to North Wales for the Welsh Round. By now very tired, he took 33 $^{1}/_{2}$ hours for this, the toughest of the three classic rounds, but it was still an outstanding achievement, one which has not yet been repeated.

1991 was a magnificent year for Anne Stentiford. Already a member, she set a new ladies record with a round late in the season, on 21st September. Leaving Keswick at 1.40 a.m. she reached Threlkeld at 5 a.m. and Dunmail Raise at 8.45 a.m., much of this still being in the dark. The big central section to Wasdale was accomplished in three minutes over five hours and Anne drove herself on to reach Honister just after 6 p.m. and return to Keswick at 8.39. Her elapsed time was 18 hours 49 minutes, a great achievement; especially as only a month earlier she had broken the existing record for the tough Paddy Buckley Round in Snowdonia with a time of 19 hours 19 minutes, nearly an hour faster than Helen Diamantides' previous record. "It was a great relief to finish" she said, "and after lots of hugs and congratulations I sat down with a can of Guinness".

"Old age hath yet his honour"

The symmetry for which Graham aimed by tackling 42 peaks at the age of 42 has resulted in yet another manifestation of the human spirit; the resolve not to concede too much to advancing years. Edward Hill in 1977 was the first to demonstrate this Peter Pan syndrome by completing a round of 50 tops at the age of 50. He was followed by Don Talbot in 1982, Tom Sykes and Peter Parkin in 1983 and Alan Barber in 1987. In the next year George Brass raised the game by doing 55 tops at the age of 50. In 1993 Paul Murray and Dennis Lucas each did a '50 at 50' and both went on five years later to do a '55 at 55'. Yiannis Tridimas became a member of the Bob Graham Club in 1995 by doing 50 tops at the age of 50, the only one so far with that distinction.

Ralph Stephenson in 1994; Peter Simpson in 1998 and Mike Sadula in 1999 kept the '50 at 50' tradition alive. All these fine rounds were done as extensions of the Bob Graham Round. Barry Johnson was the first to break away from the constraints of the round by completing a linear route from Loweswater of 55 tops at the age of 55. Joss Naylor celebrated his 60th year by a linear traverse of 60 tops in less than 36 hours. The law of diminishing returns must take effect at some point in this astonishing development, but we may not have seen the end-point yet. There are no fixed ground rules. Each attempt is a personal challenge and a private celebration. The choice of tops and starting points is a matter for each individual. Inevitably the judgment and approbation of fellow Club members will temper the final decision.

Up to now it had been only the men who had sought to push against the age barrier. In 1996 Sandra Wilkinson attempted her '50 at 50' but was forced to retire after a fall. Wendy Dodds had planned her attempt for 2001 but had to postpone it because of the foot and mouth outbreak. She took up the challenge again the next year at the age of 51 and at 9.38 pm on June 8th sprinted up to the Moot Hall having run over 53 tops in 22 hours 38 minutes, to become the first woman to join this very special band of mountain runners, and the oldest woman to have completed a Bob Graham round. That her time, including 11 extra tops, was nearly an hour faster than her original round, way back in 1979, gave her great satisfaction. "It really was much easier," she said.

The story will continue: the challenge is still there, and however much standards of fitness may rise, it is still a very fine achievement to do as Bob Graham did so long ago and stand on all of those 42 peaks within a 24-hour period. Graham's original inspiration and the enthusiasm of those who have followed him and made the Club what it is, ensure that the round continues to be a very special challenge, and the Bob Graham 24-Hour Club a very special Club.

Outstanding Achievement of the Year by a Club Member

This award was presented by Fred and Margaret Rogerson and Alan Heaton in 1982. The purpose of the Award was twofold. Firstly, to mark 21 years of friendship and memorable endeavour (1960-81) within the Lake District and over the Pennine Way. Secondly, to record members' noteworthy achievements, anywhere within the British Isles. The achievement had to be at least equal to the Bob Graham Round in distance, and only members of the Bob Graham Club were eligible for the Award.

Achievement of the Year Award: the Winners

1981/82	Geoff Bell	Pennine Way solo: 4 days 20 hrs 49 mins
1982/83	Wendy Dodds	Paddy Buckley Round; 47 tops in 25 hrs 38
1983/84	John Middleton	All the Welsh 2000 ft tops
1984/85	Mike Cudahy	Pennine Way Record; 2 days 21 hrs 54 mins
1985/86	Alan Heaton	All 214 Wainwright tops in 9 days 16 hrs 42 mins
1986/87	Joss Naylor	All 214 Wainwright tops in 7 days 1 hr 25 mins
1987/88	Martin Stone	26 Lochaber Munros in 23 hrs 24 mins
1988/89	Mark McDermott	Lake District 24 Hr Fell Record: 76 tops; 23 hrs 26 mins
1989/90	Mike Hartley	Pennine Way Record; 2 days 17 hrs 20 mins
1990/91	Robin Price	Pennine Way Double; 10 days 5 hrs 55 mins
1991/92	Anne Stentiford	Paddy Buckley Round; 19 hrs 19 mins (record) Bob Graham Round; 18 hrs 49 mins (Women's record)

1992/93	Helene Diamantides	Dragon's Back race; 38 hrs 38 mins
	Martin Stone	Dragon's Back race; 38 hrs 38 mins
1993/94	Alison Crabb	Winter Bob Graham Round in 23 hrs 52 mins
1994/95	Anne Stentiford	Women's 24 Hr Fell record 62 tops 23 hrs 17m
1995/96	Ronald Turnbull	The Donalds; 148 tops, 450 miles, 97,000 ft; 9 days 14 hrs 25 mins (record)
1996/97	no nominations	
1997/98	Mark Hartell	Lake District 24 Hr Fell Record: 77 tops; 23-47
1998/99	Yiannis Tridimas	Meirionydd Round; 47 tops in 23 hrs 32 mins
1999/00	Mark Hartell	Bob Graham Round; 14 hrs 54 mins
2000/01	Gary Byers	60 Lakeland tops; 23 hrs 40 mins

Other Notable Achievements in Lakeland 1993-2000

1993	Andrew Chamings	Paraplegic BGR;	79 hrs 3 mins
1993	Dennis Lucas	50 at 50;	23 hrs 25 mins
1993	Paul Murray	50 at 50;	22 hrs 12 mins
1997	Paul Murray	55 at 55;	23 hrs 24 mins
1998	Brian Leathley	BGR at the age of	66 yrs 352 days
1998	Nicky Lavery	Winter BGR;	22 hrs 45 mins
1998	Denis Lucas	55 at 55;	23 hrs 36 mins
1998	Peter Simpson	50 at 50;	23 hrs 37 mins
1999	Mike Sadula	50 at 50;	23 hrs 32 mins

Eric Beard on his record 56 peaks run, 1963. Eric Beard, Des Oliver, Stan Bradshaw, Alan Heaton, Ken Heaton. (Supplied by Fred Rogerson)

Left to Right: Stanley Bradshaw, Brian Leathley, Colin Henson and Donald Talbot. (F. Rogerson, 1998)

THE BOB GRAHAM 24 HOUR CLUB

By Brian Covell

As you have read earlier, Bob Graham's round of 42 peaks within 24 hours remained unsurpassed until 1960. In that year Alan Heaton traversed the same peaks in a faster time, though in the reverse direction. The enthusiasm and record-breaking performances of Alan, his brother Kenneth and Stanley Bradshaw, all members of Clayton-le-Moors Harriers, and their encouragement to others, sowed the seeds for the formation of a very remarkable club.

By the end of 1970 there were still only four people, the three mentioned above and Eric Beard, who had achieved the 42-peak round or a superior feat. On 22nd January 1971 a reunion dinner for all associated with the Lake District fell record was held at the Old Dungeon Ghyll Hotel in Langdale. Fred Rogerson, who with his wife Margaret assisted at many record attempts, proposed that a club or association be formed. This gained unanimous approval and a committee was formed with Fred as Chairman, Kenneth Heaton as Secretary and Treasurer, and six members, Stanley Bradshaw, Maurice Collett, Harry Griffin, Alan Heaton, Des Oliver and Paul Stewart.

Andrew Chamings on Kneewrecker Ridge

The first committee meeting was held later that year and it was agreed that the new club should be called "The Bob Graham 24 Hour Club." The club's aims were stated as being:

* to specify and define the 42 summits traversed by Bob Graham during his round of the fells within 24 hours,
* to provide intending qualifying members with all details and relevant information,
* to encourage and advise intending members before, and possibly during attempts,
* to record in detail all registered attempts.

Harry Griffin and Russell Thomas (1000th member)
(Brian Covell)

These objectives have remained unchanged and are now part of the club's constitution. The inaugural meeting also decided that full membership should be granted to any person traversing on foot all the 42 summits specified, within 24 hours, starting and finishing at the Moot Hall, Keswick, and that associate members be elected at the discretion of the committee. It was further decided that the holder of the 24-hour fell record should be president of the club.

In 1973 the committee decided that full membership be extended to include any person who completed a round within 24 hours, based on Graham's round but including other peaks, which at the discretion of the committee "constitutes a more meritorious achievement, either by reason of extra peaks climbed, height ascended or time taken."

The formation of the club and the many related articles written by Harry Griffin appear to have persuaded others to attempt the round and by the end of 1976 a total of 55 had successfully completed the challenge. The following year Jean Dawes of Kendal became the first lady member when she ran into Keswick after a circuit lasting 23 hours 27 minutes. Since Jean's outstanding performance a further 93 ladies have attained full membership.

During the next two years the number of full members doubled and the following decade produced a huge rise in membership. From 1981 to 1990 an average of 52 were successful each year with the peak year being 1989 when 79 completed the round. Over the following ten years the average remained high at 48 per year and in

Mark Hartell, Lake District 24 Hour Fell Record Holder and Club President

1996 the 1000th member was recorded. Contenders come from all parts of the British Isles though the majority are from Cumbria, Lancashire and Yorkshire where fell-running is particularly strong. Four members are from overseas, Reinhard Ackermann from Switzerland, John Fitch and Tony Henry from New Zealand and Ton Peters from Holland.

The ages of members varies widely with the age-group 30 to 39 being the most common. Special mention must be made of the youngest and oldest. Ben Squibb from Cornwall was 13 years and 7 months when he completed the round in 1992, and 19-year old Alison Wright from Poynton became the youngest female in 1985. Brian Leathley was 13 days short of his 67th birthday when he achieved success and Joyce Dodd at 49 is the oldest female on the day of attainment. The legendary Stanley Bradshaw of Padiham, the second member of the Bob Graham Club, celebrated his 65th birthday with a second round, beating the 24-hour limit by a few seconds.

The Bob Graham Round is not competitive in the sense of having winners and losers, but there have been many outstanding performances which are worthy of note. The fastest time for the round at the first attempt is 14 hours 56 minutes by Stuart Bland of Borrowdale, and the fastest overall time is held by Billy Bland, also from Borrowdale, who recorded 13 hours 54 minutes in 1982. Amongst the ladies Ros Coats is the fastest "first-timer" with 20 hours 31 minutes, while the best ever female time is 18 hours 49 minutes by Anne Stentiford of Biddulph in 1991. Notable veteran performers are Alan Barber, Wendy Dodds, Ed Hill, Dennis Lucas, Paul Murray, Peter Parkin, Mike Sadula, Peter Simpson, Tom Sykes and Donald Talbot, who all marked their 50th year by traversing 50 peaks, including the Bob Graham 42, in 24 hours. 55 peaks at age 55 have also been achieved by Dennis Lucas, Paul Murray and the late George Brass. Alison Crabb made a winter round in 1993 with 8 minutes to spare and 1996 saw the unusual event of twin sisters completing the long journey when Margaret Huyton and Mary White ran into Keswick hand in hand in 22 hours 31 minutes. The 24-hour fell-running record, described earlier, is 77 summits by Mark Hartell of Macclesfield Harriers in 1997, and Anne Stentiford holds the ladies record with 62 summits in 1994.

In 1982 an "Achievement of the Year" award was established by Fred and Margaret Rogerson and Alan Heaton. A trophy has been awarded to a club member who, in the opinion of a panel, has achieved the most outstanding feat of endurance similar in nature to, or greater than, the Bob Graham round. A list of winners of this trophy can be seen elsewhere in this booklet.

Every two years in the month of October the club hosts a reunion dinner dance held for many years at the Shap Wells Hotel. The reunions are very popular and provide the opportunity for members to meet and reminisce about their great days in the hills, and are always well attended. New members are presented with certificates and other awards are made. In 1980 the club was honoured to have as a special guest Phil Davidson, who accompanied Bob Graham on his record run. Phil's recollections of that tremendous feat enthralled everyone present.

Three recent reunions have proved memorable for very different reasons. In 1994 a presentation of Associate Membership was made to Andrew and Louise Chamings of York. Seventeen years earlier Andrew suffered a serious spinal injury which rendered him a paraplegic. With the aid of elbow crutches and callipers Andrew covered the Bob Graham round in 79 hours 3 minutes, spread over 10 days, accompanied by his wife. His clockwise journey included the descent of Hall's Fell ridge on Blencathra. A huge and prolonged burst of applause greeted this very special couple.

Two years later the club welcomed its 1000th member in the person of Russell Thomas from Bradford. A presentation was made to Russell by Harry Griffin who recalled the early days of the club and his meetings with Bob Graham.

The 1998 reunion marked the end of an era when Fred Rogerson, the chairman of the club since its inception, stood down from this position. Fred virtually created the club and has been the inspiration and driving force behind it. He and his wife Margaret have supported and encouraged numerous contenders, in all weathers and at all times of the day and night, for no tangible reward. A wonderful couple whose selflessness and dedication over nearly forty years have touched the lives of so many. To mark Fred's retirement the club compiled a book containing articles, letters and poems as a tribute to Fred which was presented by Mark Hartell, the club's president. Selwyn Wright, the new chairman, presented him with an inscribed Darlington crystal tankard. The ovation which followed the presentations was spontaneous and prolonged. Many hardened fell-runners were moved to tears. This most poignant occasion was tinged with the great sadness that Fred's beloved wife, who died three years earlier, was not present to share the moment with him.

One of the tributes was a poem by the late Chris Bland entitled "A Way of Life." The last verse reads:

In this life there are givers and takers,

You Fred and dear Margaret too

Have given us more than you'll ever know,

God bless and thank you,

A beautiful way of life.

And so this very special club continues to grow and flourish. Members are united by their love of the hills and their successful accomplishment of a unique and arduous physical and mental achievement. Bob Graham, whose phenomenal exploit over 70 years ago set a formidable precedent, would doubtless have been delighted that so many have literally followed in his footsteps.

Current Officers

President	Mark Hartell
Chairman	Selwyn Wright
Secretary	Morgan Williams, 6 Westville Avenue, Ilkley LS29 9AH
Membership Secretary	Brian Covell, 26 Westwood Avenue, Kendal LA9 5BB
Treasurer	Martin Hudson
Committee	John Brockbank, Jon Broxap, Peter Dawes, Wendy Dodds, Fred Rogerson